FETHIYE & OLUDENIZ

Vacation Guide

2025

A Complete Pocket Guide to Must-See Attractions,
Romantic Getaways and Outdoor Adventures on
Turkey's Mediterranean coastline

Wendy T. Sierra

Copyright

©[2025][Wendy T. Sierra]

Table of Contents

Forward

There's something truly special about discovering a place that takes your breath away—where turquoise waters meet golden sands, where history whispers through ancient ruins, and where adventure and relaxation exist in perfect harmony. Fethiye and Ölüdeniz are exactly that kind of place.

From the moment I first set foot in this enchanting region, I knew it was somewhere that would stay with me forever. The sight of the Blue Lagoon shimmering under the sun, the thrill of paragliding over dramatic cliffs, the peacefulness of watching a sunset from a secluded cove—these moments aren't just experiences; they're memories that shape the way we see the world.

This guide is more than just a collection of travel tips and recommendations. It's an invitation to explore, to wander, and to fall in love with a destination that has captured the hearts of travelers for generations. Whether you're coming for the adventure, the history, the food, or simply to escape into nature's beauty, Fethiye and Ölüdeniz promise to exceed your expectations.

In these pages, I've compiled everything you need to make your trip unforgettable—from must-see attractions to hidden gems, from thrilling outdoor activities to peaceful relaxation spots. I want you to feel prepared, inspired, and most importantly, excited about your journey. Because traveling isn't just about seeing new places; it's about experiencing them, feeling their rhythm, and making connections that last long after you've returned home.

But beyond the itineraries and insider tips, I encourage you to embrace the unexpected. Some of the best moments happen when you let go of the plan and simply follow where the road—or the waves—take you. Let yourself be drawn into the charm of a local market, take the long way back from a hike just to see where the trail leads, or spend an extra hour at a café just to soak in the atmosphere. These small, spontaneous decisions often lead to the most unforgettable stories.

So, as you turn the pages of this guide and start planning your adventure, I hope you feel the excitement building. Because you're not just visiting a destination—you're about to experience a place that will stay with you forever.

Welcome to Fethiye and Ölüdeniz. Your adventure starts here.

Introduction

Picture this: golden beaches kissed by turquoise waters, rugged mountains draped in lush greenery, ancient ruins whispering tales of forgotten civilizations, and a charming seaside town brimming with culture and adventure. This is **Fethiye and Ölüdeniz**—a sun-drenched paradise on Turkey's southwestern coast that never ceases to amaze.

As someone who craves both relaxation and adventure, I can confidently say that this destination offers the best of both worlds. Whether you're dreaming of floating over the iconic Blue Lagoon in a paraglider, sailing through hidden coves on a traditional wooden gulet, or simply unwinding on a pristine beach with the sound of gentle waves, Fethiye and Ölüdeniz have something magical in store for you.

And the best part? **2025 is the perfect time to visit!** With exciting new experiences, improved travel facilities, and fewer crowds than over-touristed hotspots, this slice of Turkey's Turquoise Coast is waiting to sweep you off your feet. So, let's dive into everything you need to know to plan an unforgettable trip.

Overview of Fethiye and Ölüdeniz

Nestled along Turkey's Mediterranean coastline, **Fethiye** is a vibrant harbor town with a unique blend of history, culture, and natural beauty. Once an important Lycian city, Fethiye now charms visitors with its bustling markets, waterfront promenade, and access to some of Turkey's most breathtaking landscapes.

Just a short drive from Fethiye, **Ölüdeniz** is home to one of the most photographed beaches in the world—the famous **Blue Lagoon**. This tranquil bay, with its crystal-clear waters and stunning mountain backdrop, is a paradise for beach lovers, adventure seekers, and nature enthusiasts alike.

Together, these two destinations form the ultimate **Turkish Riviera getaway**, offering everything from sun-soaked relaxation to adrenaline-pumping adventures. And with a rich history dating back to the Lycian, Roman, and Ottoman eras, every corner has a story to tell.

Why Visit Fethiye and Ölüdeniz in 2025?

Spectacular Natural Beauty: If you're a nature lover, prepare to be mesmerized. Fethiye and Ölüdeniz are blessed with some of Turkey's most breathtaking landscapes—dramatic cliffs, hidden coves, lush pine forests, and waters so blue they seem unreal. Whether you're hiking through Saklıkent Gorge, paragliding over Babadağ Mountain, or taking a boat trip to the Butterfly Valley, every view is postcard-perfect.

Adventure Awaits: Are you an adrenaline junkie? You're in for a treat. Ölüdeniz is world-famous for **paragliding**, offering one of the best tandem flights in the world. Imagine soaring high above the lagoon, feeling the rush of the wind while taking in panoramic views of the coastline. If heights aren't your thing, you can go scuba diving, snorkeling, or kayaking in the crystal-clear waters.

Rich History and Culture: Fethiye is a treasure trove for history buffs. Explore the **Lycian Rock Tombs**, carved into the cliffs thousands of years ago, or visit the hauntingly beautiful **Kayaköy Ghost Village**, an abandoned Greek settlement frozen in time. You can also wander through the ruins of Tlos, one of the oldest Lycian cities, where mythology and history intertwine.

Vibrant Markets and Delicious Food: One of my favorite things about Fethiye is its bustling bazaars. The Tuesday Market is a must-visit, offering everything from fresh produce to handmade souvenirs. And let's not forget the food—think sizzling kebabs, fresh seafood, mezes bursting with flavor, and the flakiest baklava you'll ever taste.

Perfect Mix of Relaxation and Adventure: Whether you want to sip a cocktail by the beach or embark on a multi-day sailing adventure, Fethiye and Ölüdeniz cater to every kind of traveler. It's the ideal place to unplug, recharge, and make unforgettable memories.

Best Time to Visit

Spring (April – June): Perfect for Exploring and Adventure

Spring is one of the best times to visit. The weather is pleasant (around **20–28°C/68–82°F**), the landscapes are lush, and the crowds are minimal. It's the ideal season for hiking the Lycian Way, exploring ancient ruins, and **paragliding** in perfect wind conditions.

Summer (July – August): Beach Bliss and Bustling Vibes

If you love hot weather and lively energy, summer is for you. Expect temperatures around **30–40°C (86–104°F)**, perfect for sunbathing, swimming, and enjoying beach parties. However, it's also the busiest time, so booking accommodations and tours in advance is a must.

Autumn (September – October): Ideal for a Balanced Getaway

For warm seas, fewer crowds, and great deals, autumn is fantastic. With temperatures ranging from **22–32°C (72–90°F)**, you can enjoy all outdoor activities without the intense summer heat. The sea is still warm, making it perfect for boat trips and swimming.

Winter (November – March): Tranquil and Budget-Friendly

Though many beach resorts wind down for the season, Fethiye remains charming in winter. With mild temperatures **(10–20°C / 50–68°F)**, you can explore historical sites, go on nature walks, and enjoy the town's laid-back vibe. It's a great option for travelers looking for a quiet, budget-friendly escape.

How to Get There

By Air: The Easiest Option

The nearest airport is **Dalaman Airport (DLM)**, located **about 45 minutes from Fethiye**. It receives **international and domestic flights** from major cities across Europe and Turkey. Once you land, you can reach Fethiye or Ölüdeniz by:

- **Shuttle Buses:** The most budget-friendly option, running regularly between Dalaman Airport and Fethiye.
- **Private Transfers:** Convenient and comfortable, ideal for groups or travelers with lots of luggage.
- **Taxis:** Readily available but slightly pricier than shuttles.

By Bus: A Scenic Journey

Turkey has an excellent intercity bus network, and you can reach Fethiye from major cities like Istanbul, Ankara, and Antalya. The ride from

Istanbul takes about **12 hours**, but **luxury buses** make it a surprisingly comfortable experience.

By Car: Ultimate Flexibility

If you love road trips, renting a car is a fantastic way to explore the region at your own pace. The coastal drive from **Antalya to Fethiye** is especially stunning, with breathtaking views of the Mediterranean.

By Boat: A Unique Arrival Experience

For a truly unforgettable entry, consider taking a Blue Cruise along the Turkish Riviera. Many gulet cruises stop in Fethiye, allowing you to sail into paradise in style.

There's something about **Fethiye and Ölüdeniz** that just captivates you. Maybe it's the way the mountains embrace the coastline, the warmth of the locals, or the endless adventures waiting to be discovered. Whatever it is, one thing's for sure—this is a place that stays with you long after you leave.

So, are you ready to explore? **Pack your bags, bring your sense of adventure, and get ready for the trip of a lifetime in 2025!**

Getting Around

Navigating Fethiye and Ölüdeniz is a breeze, thanks to their traveler-friendly layout and efficient transport options. Whether you prefer the convenience of public transportation, the freedom of a rental car, or the scenic charm of biking and walking, getting around is both simple and enjoyable. Let's break down the best ways to explore this stunning region.

Public Transportation Options

Dolmuş (Mini buses): Dolmuş is the backbone of public transportation in Fethiye and Ölüdeniz. These shared mini buses operate on fixed routes and are an affordable and reliable way to get around. You'll recognize them by their brightly colored signs displaying their destinations.

- **Routes:** Popular routes include Fethiye to Ölüdeniz, Fethiye to Kayaköy (a charming ghost village), and Fethiye to Hisarönü (a lively tourist hub).
- **Schedule:** Dolmuşes run frequently from early morning until late at night during the high season (April to October). In the low season, services may be less frequent.

- **Fares:** Expect to pay around 40-50 TL for a one-way ride between Fethiye and Ölüdeniz. Payments are made in cash directly to the driver.

Taxis: Taxis are plentiful and convenient for short trips or when traveling with heavy luggage. Look for official yellow taxis with meters.

- **Fares:** A typical ride between Fethiye and Ölüdeniz costs around 400 TL, depending on traffic and time of day.
- **Tips:** Always confirm that the meter is running or agree on a fare beforehand.

Boat Services: During the summer months, boat taxis operate between Fethiye, Ölüdeniz, and other coastal spots. These are not only practical but also offer scenic views of the coastline.

- **Popular Routes:** Fethiye to Butterfly Valley and island-hopping tours
- **Fares:** Prices vary depending on the route but typically start at 500 TL for a round trip.

Car Rentals and Driving Tips

Why Rent a Car?: If you want to explore beyond Fethiye and Ölüdeniz, renting a car is a fantastic option. It offers the flexibility to visit hidden gems like Saklıkent Gorge, Patara Beach, and the ancient city of Tlos at your own pace.

Where to Rent:

- You'll find several reputable car rental agencies at Dalaman Airport, as well as in Fethiye town.
- Popular local agencies include Garenta and Enterprise.

Rental Costs: Prices start at around 900-1,200 TL per day for a compact car. Discounts are often available for longer rentals.

Driving Tips:

- **Road Conditions:** Roads in the region are generally well-maintained, but some coastal and mountain routes can be narrow and winding.
- **Parking:** Free and paid parking options are available in Fethiye and Ölüdeniz. Parking in Ölüdeniz near the Blue Lagoon can be limited during peak season, so arriving early is recommended.
- **Fuel Costs:** As of 2025, petrol costs around 35 TL per liter.

- **Traffic Rules:** Drive on the right side of the road. Speed limits are typically 50 km/h in towns and 90 km/h on highways.
- **Navigation:** Google Maps and local GPS apps like Yandex are reliable for navigation.

Insider Tips:

- Rent a car with full insurance coverage for peace of mind.
- Be prepared for occasional traffic in Fethiye town, especially during market days.

Biking and Walking Routes

Biking: Biking is a wonderful way to explore the scenic beauty of Fethiye and its surroundings. The region offers a mix of flat coastal paths and more challenging mountain routes for cycling enthusiasts.

- **Bike Rentals:** Available from shops in Fethiye town, with prices starting at around 150 TL per day.
- **Recommended Routes:**
  - **Fethiye to Çalış Beach:** A 5 km flat and scenic ride along the coast.
  - **Fethiye to Kayaköy:** A more challenging 8 km route with some

uphill sections, rewarded by breathtaking views and a charming village at the end.

Insider Tips:

- Early morning rides are best to avoid the heat.
- Always carry water and wear sun protection.

Walking: Fethiye and Ölüdeniz are incredibly walkable, with well-maintained paths and plenty of scenic routes.

- **Fethiye Marina to the Old Town (Paspatur):** A leisurely 15-minute walk along the harbor, lined with cafes and shops.
- **Lycian Way (Starting Point in Ovacık):** One of the world's most famous trekking routes, the Lycian Way offers stunning coastal views and historical landmarks. You can choose to hike short sections or embark on multi-day adventures.
- **Ölüdeniz Beach Walk:** Stroll along the beachfront promenade for picturesque views of the Blue Lagoon.

Insider Tips:

- Wear comfortable walking shoes, especially for hikes.
- The Lycian Way requires proper gear and preparation, so consider hiring a local guide for longer treks.

Insider Travel Hacks for Smooth Navigation

- **Dolmuş Timing:** Check with locals or your accommodation for the most up-to-date schedules, as they can vary by season.
- **Mobile Apps:** Download BiTaksi for hailing taxis and Moovit for public transport navigation.
- **Local Help:** Don't hesitate to ask locals for directions—they are usually friendly and eager to assist.

By choosing the right transportation method and planning ahead, getting around Fethiye and Ölüdeniz becomes part of the adventure itself. Whether you're cruising along coastal roads, biking through lush landscapes, or hopping on a dolmuş for a taste of local life, this stunning region is yours to explore.

Top Must-See Attractions

Exploring Fethiye and Ölüdeniz is like stepping into a treasure trove of breathtaking landscapes, charming history, and unforgettable adventures. I still remember my first visit — I was spellbound by the azure waters, ancient ruins, and lush valleys that seemed straight out of a dream. Let me take you on a vivid journey through some of the must-see attractions that have captured my heart and will surely capture yours too.

Fethiye Old Town (Paspatur)

Located in the heart of Fethiye, Paspatur, or the "Old Town," is a delightful maze of narrow streets brimming with charm and character. As I wandered through its cobblestone alleys, I was greeted by the scent of Turkish coffee wafting from cozy cafes and the vibrant colors of traditional carpets hanging from shop fronts.

The area is known for its lively atmosphere and diverse shopping options. I couldn't resist browsing through the boutique stores selling handmade jewelry, leather goods, and beautiful ceramics. Bargaining with friendly shop owners was part of the fun.

But Paspatur is more than just a shopping haven — it's a cultural gem. The historic Paspatur Mosque stands as a serene reminder of the town's Ottoman past, its tranquil courtyard offering a peaceful retreat from the bustling streets. As evening falls, the town transforms into a hub of nightlife, with charming bars and restaurants serving delicious mezes and freshly caught seafood.

- **Insider Tip:** Don't leave without trying the locally famous Paspatur Honey. And if you're a fan of authentic souvenirs, this is the place to find them.

Ölüdeniz Blue Lagoon

I can confidently say that the Blue Lagoon is one of the most beautiful places I've ever seen. The

mesmerizing turquoise waters gently lap against golden sands, framed by lush green mountains — it's no wonder this spot is often featured on postcards.

The lagoon is a haven for water lovers. I spent hours swimming in its calm, warm waters, which are perfect for families and less confident swimmers. If you're feeling adventurous, there are plenty of water sports to try, including paddleboarding and kayaking.

What truly took my experience to the next level was paragliding from Babadağ Mountain. Soaring above the lagoon, with the stunning panorama stretching beneath me, was nothing short of magical. The gentle descent gave me ample time to soak in the beauty of this natural wonder.

- **Insider Tip:** Arrive early in the morning to snag a prime spot on the beach. Entrance to the Blue Lagoon Nature Park costs around 100 TL, but it's worth every penny for the tranquility and stunning views.

Kayaköy Ghost Village

Stepping into Kayaköy was like stepping back in time. This abandoned village, with its crumbling stone houses and narrow paths, exudes a haunting yet peaceful beauty. As I wandered through the ruins, I imagined the lives of the Greek and Turkish families who once called this place home.

Kayaköy is steeped in history. Following the population exchange between Greece and Turkey in 1923, the village was left deserted. Today, it stands as a poignant reminder of the region's complex past.

The eerie silence was occasionally broken by the rustling of leaves or the chirping of birds, adding to the mystical atmosphere. I climbed to the church at the top of the hill, where stunning views of the surrounding valley rewarded my efforts.

- **Insider Tip:** Bring sturdy shoes, as the paths can be uneven. Guided tours are available if you want to delve deeper into the village's history.

Saklıkent Gorge

Imagine walking through a gorge so deep that sunlight barely touches the floor — that's Saklıkent for you. This natural wonder, one of the longest gorges in Turkey, offers a thrilling adventure for nature lovers.

I waded through icy-cold waters, feeling the rush of the current against my legs as towering cliffs rose dramatically on either side. The sheer scale of the gorge is awe-inspiring. The trail eventually led me

to serene spots where I could sit and soak in the beauty of the place.

For those seeking more adventure, there are opportunities for tubing down the river or simply splashing around in its refreshing waters.

After my trek, I indulged in a delicious meal at one of the riverside restaurants, where tables are set on wooden platforms above the flowing water. The fresh trout grilled to perfection was a highlight.

- **Insider Tip:** Wear water shoes for better grip and to protect your feet from sharp rocks. Entrance to the gorge costs around 200 TL.

Butterfly Valley (Kelebekler Vadisi)

I was captivated the moment I set eyes on Butterfly Valley. Accessible only by boat or a challenging hike, this secluded paradise is a must-visit for those seeking a slice of untouched nature.

The valley is named for the diverse species of butterflies that flutter through its lush greenery. While I didn't spot as many butterflies as I had hoped, the breathtaking scenery more than made up for it. Towering cliffs frame the valley, leading down to a pristine beach where I spent hours swimming and relaxing.

The sense of tranquility here is unparalleled. Without the distractions of modern life, I felt completely connected to nature.

For the adventurous, there's a trail that leads to a beautiful waterfall deeper into the valley. It's a bit of a scramble, but well worth the effort for the serene reward at the end.

- **Insider Tip:** Boats to Butterfly Valley depart from Ölüdeniz Beach and cost around 600 TL for a round trip. Bring plenty of water and snacks, as amenities are limited.

In a nutshell, Fethiye and Ölüdeniz offer a kaleidoscope of experiences that cater to every type of traveler. Whether you're wandering through the charming streets of Paspatur, marveling at the natural beauty of the Blue Lagoon, or uncovering the stories of Kayaköy, each moment is filled with wonder. These iconic landmarks have left an indelible mark on my heart, and I'm confident they will do the same for you. So, lace up your shoes, pack your curiosity, and get ready to create memories that will last a lifetime.

Hidden Gems for a Unique Experience

Fethiye and Ölüdeniz have so many spectacular sights that it's easy to stick to the well-trodden paths of famous beaches and historic landmarks. But I quickly learned that the real magic often lies in the lesser-known spots — the hidden gems that don't always make the guidebooks but leave an unforgettable impression. These secret havens captured my heart, and I can't wait to share them with you. Let's dive into the enchanting corners of this mesmerizing region, where adventure and tranquility await in equal measure.

Kabak Bay: A Serene Escape into Nature

If you're longing for an unspoiled paradise where time slows down and nature wraps you in its embrace, Kabak Bay is the answer. It's a bit of a journey to get there, but trust me, it's worth every step. After a winding drive through pine-covered hills, followed by a short but steep hike, I was rewarded with a breathtaking view of turquoise waters framed by lush green cliffs.

Unlike the more popular beaches, Kabak Bay has an unpolished, rustic charm. There are no sprawling resorts here — just eco-friendly bungalows and simple campsites. I spent my days swimming in the crystal-clear waters and my evenings watching the sun dip below the horizon, painting the sky in hues of orange and pink.

For the adventurous, there are plenty of hiking trails around the bay, including a section of the famous Lycian Way. The dense forest and dramatic coastal views made it one of my favorite hikes in the region.

- **Insider Tip:** Pack sturdy shoes for the hike down and plenty of water. If you're up for a digital detox, consider staying overnight at one of the rustic lodges to truly soak in the tranquility.

Afkule Monastery: A Spiritual Retreat with a View

Tucked away on a rugged cliffside, Afkule Monastery feels like a place frozen in time. As I made my way up the narrow trail, surrounded by the scent of wild herbs and the distant hum of cicadas, I couldn't help but feel a sense of reverence.

The ruins themselves are simple yet captivating, with stone arches and crumbling walls that hint at their ancient past. But what truly took my breath away was the view — an expansive panorama of the Aegean Sea stretching endlessly before me. It was easy to see why monks chose this serene spot for contemplation.

I lingered for a while, sitting on a weathered stone and soaking in the peace of the place. The only sounds were the rustling of the wind and the occasional cry of a seagull.

- **Insider Tip:** The hike to the monastery is moderately challenging, so wear sturdy shoes and bring water. Early morning or late afternoon visits are best to avoid the midday heat.

Lycian Rock Tombs: Ancient History Etched into the Cliffs

I've always been fascinated by ancient history, so the Lycian Rock Tombs were high on my list. These tombs, carved into the cliffs overlooking Fethiye, are a striking testament to the craftsmanship and spiritual beliefs of the ancient Lycians.

As I stood before the grand tomb of Amyntas, the largest and most impressive of the tombs, I marveled at the intricate details etched into the stone. It's incredible to think that these structures

have stood here for thousands of years, weathering the elements and watching over the town below.

Climbing up to the tombs was a bit of a workout, but the stunning view of Fethiye and the surrounding bay made it all worthwhile.

- **Insider Tip:** The best time to visit is late afternoon when the light is soft and golden, casting a beautiful glow over the tombs. Don't forget your camera!

Şövalye Island: A Secluded Oasis

If you're looking for a peaceful escape from the hustle and bustle, Şövalye Island is a hidden gem that promises tranquility and charm. I hopped on a

small boat from Fethiye's harbor and within minutes was stepping onto this car-free island, where life moves at a gentler pace.

The island is perfect for leisurely strolls along its scenic paths, with stunning views of the turquoise waters and lush landscapes at every turn. I stumbled upon quiet coves where I could swim undisturbed and found a charming little café serving fresh seafood with a view that's hard to beat.

What I loved most about Şövalye Island was its rich history. Ruins of ancient fortifications and stone walls hint at its past as a strategic stronghold.

Exploring these remnants felt like uncovering a secret chapter of the region's story.

- **Insider Tip:** Pack a picnic and spend the day exploring. The boat ride is affordable and frequent, making it an easy and worthwhile day trip.

Gemile Bay: A Hidden Paradise for Beach Lovers

Gemile Bay is one of those places that feels like a well-kept secret. Nestled in a picturesque cove, this secluded bay offers pristine waters, soft sands, and a backdrop of pine-covered hills.

The bay is perfect for a relaxed day by the sea. I spent hours swimming in the calm, clear waters and basking in the sun. There's a simple beachside café where I enjoyed a delicious lunch of freshly grilled fish and a refreshing glass of ayran.

What sets Gemile Bay apart is its proximity to Gemile Island, also known as St. Nicholas Island. A short boat ride takes you to this fascinating spot, where you can explore Byzantine ruins and soak in panoramic views of the surrounding coastline.

- **Insider Tip:** Visit in the early morning or late afternoon to avoid crowds. Bring snorkeling gear to explore the underwater wonders of the bay.

In summary, these hidden gems in Fethiye and Ölüdeniz offer a refreshing escape from the typical tourist trails. Whether it's the serene beauty of Kabak Bay, the spiritual solitude of Afkule Monastery, or the ancient allure of the Lycian Rock Tombs, each spot has its own unique story to tell. Exploring these off-the-beaten-path treasures made my journey even more unforgettable, and I'm confident they'll do the same for you. So, venture beyond the familiar and discover the magic that lies just beneath the surface. You won't regret it.

Outdoor Adventures and Activities

If there's one thing I discovered in Fethiye and Ölüdeniz, it's that adventure is always just around the corner. Whether soaring through the skies, exploring rugged mountain trails, or diving deep beneath the turquoise waters, this stunning region offers a playground for thrill-seekers and nature lovers alike. Every activity filled me with a rush of excitement and awe, and I can't wait to share these experiences with you.

Paragliding Over Ölüdeniz: A Bird's-Eye View of Paradise

I'll never forget the moment my feet lifted off the edge of Babadağ Mountain. A mix of exhilaration and slight nervousness washed over me as the wind carried us into the sky. Below, the shimmering Blue Lagoon of Ölüdeniz spread out like a jewel, framed by lush green hills and golden sands.

Paragliding over Ölüdeniz is often touted as one of the best experiences in the world, and I completely understand why. As I soared through the air, weightless and free, the panoramic views were simply breathtaking. The sky was painted in hues of blue, and the horizon seemed endless.

The landing was gentle, right on the sandy beach, where I was greeted by cheering onlookers. I felt an incredible sense of accomplishment and joy — it's a memory I'll carry forever.

- **Insider Tip:** Book your flight with a reputable company, and don't hesitate to ask your pilot for tricks like spirals if you're up for an extra adrenaline rush!

Hiking the Lycian Way: Trekking Through History and Natural Beauty

Lace up your hiking boots because the Lycian Way is a trekker's dream come true. Stretching over 500 kilometers along the rugged coastline, this ancient trail offers a blend of history, culture, and jaw-dropping landscapes.

While I didn't tackle the entire route, I chose a section from Fethiye to Kayaköy, and it was absolutely worth it. The trail meandered through pine forests, past ancient ruins, and along cliffs with sweeping views of the sea. I loved the sense of solitude and connection with nature.

One of the highlights was stumbling upon secluded beaches, where I could cool off with a refreshing swim. The wildflowers lining the path added bursts of color to the journey, making it feel like a scene from a postcard.

- **Insider Tip:** Spring and autumn are the best times to hike due to the mild weather. Don't forget to carry plenty of water and a good map or GPS device.

Jeep Safaris: A Wild Ride Through the Countryside

For a more rugged adventure, I hopped into a Jeep for a thrilling safari through Fethiye's countryside. This wasn't just a scenic drive — it was an exhilarating journey filled with laughter, splashes, and off-road excitement.

Our convoy roared through dirt tracks, past traditional villages and lush valleys. We made stops at beautiful spots like Saklıkent Gorge, where I waded through the icy waters of the canyon. The highlight, though, was the spontaneous water fights between Jeeps — a fun and refreshing way to beat the heat.

The safari also gave me a chance to connect with locals and enjoy a delicious traditional lunch in a charming village setting.

- **Insider Tip:** Wear clothes you don't mind getting wet and bring a sense of adventure. The water fights are all in good fun, but you'll definitely get soaked!

Scuba Diving & Snorkeling: Explore Underwater Wonderland

Fethiye's crystal-clear waters aren't just beautiful from above — they're teeming with marine life and underwater wonders. I decided to take the plunge and go scuba diving, and it turned out to be one of the most magical experiences of my trip.

The dive sites around Fethiye are diverse, from vibrant coral reefs to fascinating caves and even ancient shipwrecks. My guide led me through an underwater paradise filled with colorful fish, playful sea turtles, and swaying seagrass. The feeling of weightlessness and the serene silence of the deep blue sea were incredibly calming.

For those who prefer staying closer to the surface, snorkeling is equally rewarding. I spent hours floating above coral gardens, mesmerized by the marine life below.

- **Insider Tip:** Beginners should try the sites around Aquarium Bay, which are calm and shallow. Don't forget to bring an underwater camera!

Boat Tours and Sailing: Exploring Hidden Coves and Islands

There's something incredibly freeing about being out on the open water, with the salty breeze in your hair and the sun on your skin. Taking a boat tour was one of the best decisions I made — it gave me a chance to explore secluded coves, hidden beaches, and charming islands that aren't accessible by land.

The traditional wooden gulets, with their polished decks and comfortable seating, are the way to go. Our captain took us to some of the most beautiful spots, including Butterfly Valley and St. Nicholas Island. We anchored in calm bays where I could dive straight into the turquoise waters.

One of the most magical moments was enjoying a freshly prepared lunch onboard, surrounded by nothing but the sound of gentle waves.

- **Insider Tip:** Opt for a private boat tour if you can — it offers more flexibility and a personalized experience. Don't forget your sunscreen and a good book for those lazy moments on deck.

In summary, Fethiye and Ölüdeniz are a playground for outdoor enthusiasts and thrill-seekers. From soaring through the skies while paragliding to diving into the depths of the sea, every adventure here is filled with excitement and wonder. The natural beauty of the region adds an extra layer of magic to each experience.

Whether you're an adrenaline junkie or simply someone who loves connecting with nature, these outdoor activities will leave you with unforgettable memories. So pack your sense of adventure and get ready to experience Fethiye and Ölüdeniz in the most exhilarating way possible!

Beaches and Relaxation Spots

When I think about Fethiye and Ölüdeniz, the first thing that comes to mind is the shimmering coastline, where golden sands meet crystal-clear waters. These beaches are more than just picturesque — they're places where time slows down, and every gentle wave invites you to unwind. Whether you're looking to bask in the sun, swim in tranquil waters, or simply find a quiet spot to watch the world go by, the beaches here are a slice of paradise. Let me take you on a journey through some of my favorite serene spots.

Ölüdeniz Beach: The Jewel of the Turquoise Coast

Ölüdeniz Beach is often called one of the most beautiful beaches in the world, and I can confidently say it lives up to the hype. As I stepped onto its soft sands for the first time, the vibrant hues of blue stretching before me took my breath away. The beach curves gracefully along the coastline, with the majestic Babadağ Mountain standing proudly in the background.

The calm, clear waters are perfect for swimming, and I found myself floating effortlessly, soaking in the tranquility. Even with other beachgoers around, there's a peaceful vibe that envelops Ölüdeniz Beach.

I loved taking long walks along the shore, feeling the gentle waves lap at my feet. As the sun began to set, painting the sky with shades of pink and orange, I found a quiet spot to sit and marvel at nature's masterpiece.

- **Insider Tip:** Arrive early in the morning to claim a prime spot on the sand and enjoy the beach at its most peaceful.

Kumburnu Beach: A Tranquil Escape by the Lagoon

Just a short stroll from Ölüdeniz Beach lies Kumburnu Beach, a hidden gem nestled by the famous Blue Lagoon. The contrast between the turquoise waters of the lagoon and the lush greenery surrounding it creates a scene straight out of a postcard.

What I loved most about Kumburnu Beach was its serene atmosphere. It felt like a world away from the bustling main beach. I rented a sun lounger under a thatched umbrella and spent the afternoon reading, dozing off to the gentle sounds of the water.

The lagoon's calm waters are ideal for a leisurely swim or even paddleboarding if you're feeling adventurous. I found it hard to leave this tranquil oasis.

- **Insider Tip:** There's a small entrance fee to access the beach, but it's well worth it for the peaceful ambiance. Bring snacks and drinks if you plan to stay for a while.

Gemiler Beach: A Secluded Slice of Heaven

If you're looking to escape the crowds, Gemiler Beach is the perfect spot. Tucked away near the ancient ruins of St. Nicholas Island, this beach offers a more rustic and secluded vibe. The drive to get there is a bit adventurous, but the reward is well worth it.

The beach itself is framed by olive trees, and the water is a mesmerizing shade of blue. I found it incredibly peaceful, with only a handful of visitors scattered along the shore.

What makes Gemiler Beach truly special is the sense of history that lingers in the air. After a refreshing swim, I explored the nearby ruins, imagining what life must have been like centuries ago.

- **Insider Tip:** Pack a picnic and plenty of water, as amenities are limited. The sunsets here are spectacular, so stay until dusk if you can.

Kidrak Beach: A Quiet Gem for Nature Lovers

Just a short drive from Ölüdeniz, Kidrak Beach is a haven for those seeking a more natural and less commercialized beach experience. As I walked down the path to the beach, I was greeted by the soothing sound of waves and the scent of pine trees.

The beach is spacious, with golden sand and pebbles that glisten under the sun. I loved spreading out my towel under the shade of a tree and simply soaking in the beauty around me. The water here is clear and inviting, perfect for a refreshing swim.

Kidrak Beach felt like a retreat into nature, away from the hustle and bustle of the more popular spots. It was just me, the sea, and the gentle rustling of leaves in the breeze.

- **Insider Tip:** There's a small entrance fee, but it helps maintain the pristine condition of the beach. Don't forget to bring a hat and sunscreen, as shaded spots are limited.

The beaches of Fethiye and Ölüdeniz are more than just places to lay your towel; they're sanctuaries of peace and beauty. Each one offers a unique experience, from the vibrant energy of Ölüdeniz Beach to the tranquil escape of Gemiler and Kidrak.

As I reflect on my time here, I can still feel the warmth of the sun on my skin and hear the gentle lull of the waves. If you're seeking a destination where you can truly unwind and connect with nature, these beaches are calling your name. Trust me, you won't want to leave.

Cultural and Historical Experiences

Fethiye and its surrounding areas are rich with cultural and historical treasures waiting to be explored. As I wandered through ancient ruins, admired local crafts, and delved into the region's fascinating history, I felt a profound connection to the stories of the past and the vibrant present of this beautiful corner of Turkey. Let me take you on a journey through some of the must-visit cultural and historical gems in Fethiye.

Fethiye Museum: A Journey Through Time

Stepping into the Fethiye Museum felt like stepping back in time. This small but impressive museum offers a fascinating glimpse into the region's ancient history, showcasing artifacts from the Lycian, Roman, and Byzantine periods.

As I moved through the exhibits, I marveled at the intricate pottery, beautifully crafted jewelry, and ancient coins that once circulated in bustling markets. One of the most captivating displays was the collection of Lycian stone carvings and inscriptions, which tell tales of a civilization that once thrived in this region.

What truly stood out was the detailed sarcophagus on display, with its ornate carvings that seemed to whisper stories of the past. The museum's layout made it easy to follow the historical timeline, giving me a deeper appreciation for Fethiye's rich heritage.

- **Insider Tip:** The museum is often quiet, making it a peaceful place to explore. Don't miss the well-preserved mosaics near the entrance.

Telmessos Ancient Theatre: Echoes of the Past

Just a short walk from the town center, the Telmessos Ancient Theatre stands as a testament to Fethiye's ancient past. Built during the Roman period, this theater once hosted performances and events for up to 6,000 spectators.

As I climbed the stone steps, I couldn't help but imagine the crowds that once gathered here, their voices mingling with the sea breeze. The view from the top was breathtaking, offering a panoramic vista of Fethiye Bay.

Despite the wear of time, the theater's structure remains impressive. I found myself tracing my fingers along the weathered stones, marveling at the craftsmanship that has withstood centuries.

- **Insider Tip:** Visit in the late afternoon when the sun casts a golden glow over the ruins. Bring a camera to capture the stunning views.

Local Markets and Artisans: A Celebration of Culture

No visit to Fethiye would be complete without immersing yourself in the vibrant local markets. The bustling Fethiye Market, held every Tuesday, is a sensory delight. As I wandered through the maze of stalls, I was greeted by the enticing aroma of fresh herbs and spices, the vibrant colors of seasonal produce, and the cheerful banter of vendors.

One of my favorite finds was a stall selling handwoven textiles. The intricate patterns and vibrant colors were a testament to the region's rich artisan traditions. I couldn't resist picking up a few pieces to take home as souvenirs.

Beyond the market, Fethiye is home to talented artisans who keep traditional crafts alive. I stumbled upon a small workshop where a skilled jeweler was crafting delicate pieces inspired by ancient Lycian designs. Watching the meticulous process was mesmerizing and gave me a newfound appreciation for the craftsmanship behind these beautiful creations.

- **Insider Tip:** Don't shy away from haggling at the market — it's part of the experience. And make sure to try the local olives and freshly baked bread.

Cultural Traditions and Local Life

One of the most rewarding aspects of exploring Fethiye was getting to know the local culture. The people here are warm and welcoming, eager to share their traditions and stories.

I had the chance to participate in a traditional Turkish tea ceremony, where I learned about the significance of tea in Turkish culture. Sitting on cushions, sipping the fragrant brew, and engaging in lively conversation was a highlight of my trip.

Another memorable experience was attending a local music performance. The haunting melodies of traditional Turkish instruments filled the air, creating a magical atmosphere. It was a beautiful reminder of the region's rich cultural heritage.

- **Insider Tip:** Keep an eye out for cultural events and performances, especially during the summer months.

Fethiye offers so much more than stunning landscapes and beautiful beaches. Its cultural and historical experiences provide a deeper understanding of the region and its people. Whether you're exploring ancient ruins, marveling at artifacts in the museum, or getting lost in the vibrant market scene, you'll find yourself immersed in stories that span centuries.

Trust me, taking the time to connect with the cultural and historical heart of Fethiye will make your visit even more memorable.

Family-Friendly Activities

When it comes to planning a family vacation, Fethiye and Ölüdeniz have plenty to offer. From thrilling water parks to tranquil beaches and unforgettable nature adventures, there's no shortage of wholesome fun for parents and kids alike. I personally found these experiences not only entertaining but also perfect for creating lasting family memories.

Aqua Parks: Splashing Good Fun for Everyone

What better way to beat the Mediterranean heat than a day at an aqua park? Fethiye's water parks are a big hit with families, offering exciting slides, lazy rivers, and pools suitable for all ages. My kids absolutely loved the thrill of racing down the twisty water slides, while I found myself pleasantly relaxed floating along the lazy river.

The parks have dedicated areas for young children, complete with gentle splash zones and pint-sized slides. I appreciated the lifeguards stationed throughout the park, giving me peace of mind while the kids played.

Most parks also have shaded picnic areas, restaurants, and snack bars — perfect for recharging between all the fun.

- **Insider Tip:** Arrive early to secure a prime spot near the pool. Don't forget sunscreen and water shoes for little feet, as surfaces can get hot.

Butterfly Valley Exploration: A Natural Wonderland

Butterfly Valley is a magical spot that had my entire family in awe. Getting there was an adventure in itself — we opted for a boat ride from Ölüdeniz, which offered stunning views of the coastline.

Once we arrived, the real adventure began. The valley is home to lush greenery and, during the right season, swarms of vibrant butterflies that flit through the air like living jewels. My kids were delighted every time they spotted one resting on a leaf or fluttering nearby.

We took a gentle hike along the valley floor, where the shaded pathways kept us cool. The waterfall at the end of the trail was a refreshing reward, and the kids couldn't resist splashing around in the cool water.

- **Insider Tip:** Wear comfortable shoes for the hike and bring plenty of water. The best time to see butterflies is between June and September.

Beach Days and Safe Swimming Spots: Fun in the Sun

The beaches of Fethiye and Ölüdeniz are family-friendly havens where kids can splash, build sandcastles, and run freely. I found the calm, clear waters at several spots to be ideal for safe swimming, even for younger children.

Ölüdeniz Blue Lagoon: The tranquil waters of the lagoon are perfect for families. With no strong currents and plenty of shallow areas, I felt completely at ease letting my kids play in the water. The beach facilities, including loungers and cafés, made it easy to spend the whole day there.

Kidrak Beach: For a slightly quieter experience, Kidrak Beach offers a peaceful atmosphere and gentle waves. We packed a picnic and enjoyed a relaxed afternoon, listening to the waves and watching the kids collect seashells.

Gemiler Beach: This beach had a more rustic vibe but was equally family-friendly. The shallow waters were perfect for wading, and the lack of large crowds made it feel like our little slice of paradise.

- **Insider Tip:** Bring beach toys, snacks, and plenty of water. Look out for small cafés near popular beaches where you can grab ice cream and cold drinks.

Nature Walks and Scenic Picnics

One of the simple pleasures we enjoyed as a family was exploring Fethiye's scenic trails. The shaded pathways and gentle trails made for enjoyable walks, even with little ones in tow.

We found lovely picnic spots along the way, where we laid out a blanket, unpacked some local treats, and soaked in the beauty of nature. The kids loved spotting wildflowers and watching butterflies dance through the air.

- **Insider Tip:** The trails near Kayaköy Ghost Village are particularly scenic and family-friendly. Bring a camera to capture those picture-perfect moments.

Whether it's the thrill of an aqua park, the wonder of exploring Butterfly Valley, or the simple joy of a beach day, Fethiye and Ölüdeniz have something for every family. I found these experiences not only fun but also enriching — moments where we could connect as a family and create lasting memories. If you're looking for a destination that caters to all ages with a blend of adventure and relaxation, this is it. Trust me, your kids will thank you for it!

Romantic Experiences for Couples

There's something undeniably enchanting about Fethiye and Ölüdeniz, where breathtaking landscapes and serene seascapes set the stage for unforgettable romantic moments. Whether you're celebrating an anniversary, honeymooning, or simply seeking to rekindle your connection, this beautiful part of Turkey offers countless opportunities for love to blossom. From dreamy sunset cruises to intimate dining experiences, let me share how this captivating destination can sweep you off your feet.

Sunset Cruises: Sailing Into Romance

Few things are as romantic as gliding across calm turquoise waters, hand in hand with your partner, as the sun paints the sky in hues of gold and crimson. My partner and I booked a private sunset cruise, and it was one of the most magical experiences we've ever shared.

The boat gently rocked as we sipped on chilled wine, the sea breeze brushing against our faces. The captain steered us toward quiet coves, away from the bustling shorelines, allowing us to fully immerse ourselves in the tranquil beauty of the moment. As the sun dipped below the horizon, casting shimmering reflections across the water, I couldn't help but feel like we were the only two people in the world.

- **Insider Tip:** Many operators offer customizable packages, including dinner on board. Bring a light jacket for when the breeze picks up after sunset.

Secluded Beach Picnics: A Taste of Paradise

For a truly intimate experience, nothing beats a secluded beach picnic. We packed a basket filled with local delights — freshly baked bread, savory cheeses, juicy olives, and a bottle of crisp white wine. Gemiler Bay was our chosen spot, a hidden gem with soft sands and crystal-clear waters.

We laid out a blanket under the shade of a pine tree, the gentle lapping of waves creating a soothing soundtrack. Time seemed to stand still as we laughed, shared stories, and savored the simple joy of being together. After our meal, we strolled along the shoreline, leaving footprints in the sand as the sun cast a warm glow over the bay.

- **Insider Tip:** For an extra touch of romance, arrange your picnic during the late afternoon to catch the sunset. Don't forget to bring a portable speaker for some soft music.

Romantic Dining Spots: A Feast for the Senses

Fethiye and Ölüdeniz are home to a variety of charming restaurants that cater perfectly to couples seeking a romantic night out. One evening, we dined at a cozy hillside restaurant overlooking the bay. The candlelight ambiance, combined with the gentle sounds of the sea below, made for an unforgettable setting.

We savored every bite of our meal, from freshly grilled seafood to decadent desserts. The highlight was the impeccable service — the staff went above and beyond to make us feel special, even surprising us with a complimentary dessert adorned with sparklers.

For a different vibe, we also tried a beachside restaurant in Ölüdeniz. With our toes in the sand and the stars twinkling overhead, it was a quintessential Mediterranean dining experience.

Recommended Spots:

- **Yacht Classic Restaurant (Fethiye):** Ideal for an elegant dinner with stunning waterfront views.
- **Jade Terrace (Ölüdeniz):** Perfect for dining under the stars with a relaxed ambiance.
- **Mozaik Bahçe (Fethiye):** For a garden setting with authentic Turkish cuisine.

Insider Tip: Reserve a table in advance, especially during peak season. Opt for outdoor seating to make the most of the beautiful views.

Shared Adventures: Bonding Through Exploration

While relaxation is key to any romantic getaway, sharing adventures can deepen your connection. We hiked a portion of the Lycian Way, pausing at scenic viewpoints to catch our breath and marvel at the awe-inspiring landscapes. There was something exhilarating about conquering the trail together, knowing we'd have stories to share for years to come.

Another highlight was a tandem paragliding experience over Ölüdeniz. Soaring through the sky, with the turquoise lagoon shimmering below, was both thrilling and surreal. The sense of freedom and wonder made it a moment we'll never forget.

- **Insider Tip:** If paragliding isn't your thing, a leisurely boat tour exploring hidden coves and pristine beaches can be just as memorable.

Fethiye and Ölüdeniz offer endless opportunities for couples to connect, celebrate love, and create cherished memories. Whether you're sailing into the sunset, dining under the stars, or simply walking hand in hand along a quiet beach, every moment here feels infused with magic. Trust me, these experiences will leave you both longing to return again and again.

Dining and Local Cuisine

One of the greatest joys of visiting Fethiye and Ölüdeniz is indulging in the rich and flavorful Turkish cuisine. The region's dining scene perfectly captures the essence of Mediterranean and Middle Eastern flavors, offering everything from traditional dishes prepared with love to innovative takes on Turkish classics. Whether you're savoring a meal at a beachfront café, grabbing a quick bite at a street food stall, or indulging in a fine dining experience, the culinary delights here will leave you craving more. Let me guide you through the must-try dishes, top restaurants, and hidden foodie gems in Fethiye and Ölüdeniz.

Must-Try Turkish Dishes: A Feast of Flavors

Turkish cuisine is a celebration of bold spices, fresh ingredients, and hearty flavors. Here are some dishes that you absolutely cannot miss:

Meze Platters: Start any meal with a selection of meze — small plates that are perfect for sharing. From creamy hummus to spicy ezme (tomato and pepper dip) and dolma (stuffed grape leaves), every bite is a burst of flavor. Paired with freshly baked bread, it's the perfect introduction to Turkish dining.

Pide: Often referred to as Turkish pizza, pide is a boat-shaped flatbread topped with ingredients like minced meat, spinach, cheese, or egg. I found it to be both filling and delicious, especially when paired with a side of ayran, a refreshing yogurt-based drink.

Kebab Varieties: Turkish kebabs are legendary, and for good reason. Whether it's the smoky Adana kebab (spicy minced meat), the tender shish kebab, or the hearty Iskender kebab served with yogurt and tomato sauce, each variation is a delight for the senses.

Gözleme: A simple yet satisfying dish, gözleme is a thin, hand-rolled pastry filled with cheese, spinach, or minced meat, then cooked on a griddle. It's a popular street food snack and pairs wonderfully with a cup of Turkish tea.

Lokma and Baklava: No meal is complete without dessert, and Turkey offers some of the best. Lokma are bite-sized doughnuts soaked in syrup, while baklava is a rich pastry layered with nuts and honey. Both are indulgent and irresistible.

Best Restaurants in Fethiye and Ölüdeniz

Dining in Fethiye and Ölüdeniz is as much about the ambiance as it is about the food. Here are some of my favorite spots:

Yacht Classic Restaurant (Fethiye): Set right by the marina, this upscale restaurant is perfect for a romantic evening or a special occasion. Their seafood dishes, especially the grilled sea bass, are a must-try. The sunset views over the water make the experience even more magical.

Buzz Beach Bar (Ölüdeniz): With its laid-back vibe and beachfront location, Buzz Beach Bar is an excellent spot for a relaxed meal. The menu features a mix of Turkish and international dishes, but their meze platter and lamb shank are standout options.

Mozaik Bahçe (Fethiye): Tucked away in the heart of Fethiye, this charming garden restaurant specializes in traditional Hatay cuisine. The flavors are rich and authentic, and their slow-cooked lamb tandir is phenomenal.

The Olive Garden (Kabak Bay): If you venture out to Kabak Bay, make time for a meal at The Olive Garden. The panoramic views of the valley and sea are worth the trip alone, and the food — from freshly caught fish to hearty vegetarian dishes — is exceptional.

Street Food Spots and Local Delicacies

Street food in Fethiye and Ölüdeniz is a fantastic way to experience local flavors without breaking the bank. I spent many afternoons wandering through markets and streets, sampling delicious snacks along the way.

Çalış Beach Night Market: Here, you'll find everything from savory gözleme to grilled corn on the cob. I loved trying the midye dolma (stuffed mussels) — a local delicacy that's packed with seasoned rice and served with a squeeze of lemon.

Fethiye Fish Market: This vibrant market is a foodie's paradise. Choose your seafood fresh from the stalls and have it cooked to perfection at one of the nearby restaurants. The grilled octopus and jumbo prawns are not to be missed.

Simit Stalls: Simit, often referred to as the: Turkish bagel, is a popular street food snack. The sesame-covered bread rings are perfect for a quick breakfast or a mid-morning bite.

Lokma Stalls: You can't visit Fethiye without trying lokma. Watching the street vendors expertly fry these golden dough balls before drenching them in syrup is an experience in itself.

Beachfront Cafés: Dining with a View

For a truly relaxing meal, there's nothing quite like dining at a beachfront café, with the sound of waves gently lapping in the background.

Sea Horse Beach Club (Ölüdeniz): This family-friendly spot offers a mix of Turkish and international dishes, with plenty of shaded seating right by the water. Their grilled calamari and fresh salads are perfect for a light lunch.

Help Beach & Yacht Club (Fethiye): Set on a private beach, this chic café-restaurant serves gourmet dishes in a stunning setting. I recommend the seafood pasta and the signature cocktails.

Sugar Beach Club (Ölüdeniz): Known for its laid-back vibe, Sugar Beach Club serves everything from hearty breakfasts to wood-fired pizzas. It's a great place to spend the day lounging by the sea before enjoying a casual dinner.

The dining experiences in Fethiye and Ölüdeniz are as diverse as the region itself. Whether you're savoring traditional Turkish dishes, exploring street food markets, or enjoying a candlelit meal by the sea, every bite tells a story of rich culinary heritage and fresh, local ingredients. Trust me, the food here is more than just a meal — it's an adventure in its own right.

Nightlife & Entertainment

As the sun dips below the horizon, Fethiye and Ölüdeniz come alive with vibrant nightlife and energetic entertainment. Whether you're in the mood for sophisticated cocktails at a chic lounge, dancing barefoot under the stars at a beach party, or soaking up live music vibes, this stunning coastal region knows how to keep the fun going well into the night. Let me guide you through some of the best spots and experiences to enjoy after dark.

Bars and Lounges: Sip and Socialize in Style

If you enjoy a relaxed vibe with expertly crafted drinks, Fethiye and Ölüdeniz offer a variety of bars and lounges to suit your mood.

Help Beach Bar (Ölüdeniz): This trendy beachfront bar combines tropical vibes with creative cocktails. The laid-back ambiance makes it perfect for sipping on a mojito while gazing out at the moonlit waves. If you're hungry, their gourmet bar bites will keep you satisfied.

Deep Blue Bar (Fethiye): A favorite among both locals and travelers, Deep Blue Bar is known for its friendly atmosphere and great music selection. I loved how the staff made everyone feel welcome, and their signature gin and tonic is a must-try.

Fethiye Marina Yacht Club: For a more sophisticated experience, head to the Fethiye Marina Yacht Club. With its elegant setting overlooking the boats, it's an excellent spot for a sunset drink or a late-night glass of wine.

The Reef Bar (Çalış Beach): This beachside gem is the ideal place to unwind with a cocktail as the sound of waves creates the perfect background music. Their passion fruit margarita is a crowd-pleaser.

Live Music Venues: Feel the Rhythm of the Region

Music lovers will find plenty of venues offering live performances, ranging from mellow acoustic sets to energetic rock bands.

Car Cemetery Bar (Fethiye): Don't let the name fool you — Car Cemetery Bar is one of the liveliest spots in town. With its eclectic decor and fantastic live music, it's a great place to let loose and enjoy the night. The bands often play a mix of rock, blues, and Turkish classics.

Kumsal Pide (Ölüdeniz): By day, Kumsal Pide serves some of the best Turkish comfort food in town. By night, it transforms into a cozy live music venue. I loved the intimate vibe and the talented local musicians who perform here regularly.

Barumba Bar (Fethiye): Barumba is a go-to for those who enjoy a mix of music genres and a lively crowd. Their themed nights, often featuring live DJ performances, make every visit unique.

Jazz Bar (Fethiye): For a more relaxed evening, Jazz Bar offers soothing jazz and blues performances. The atmosphere is intimate, and the cocktails are expertly crafted.

Beach Parties: Dance Under the Stars

If you're looking for high-energy fun, the beach parties in Fethiye and Ölüdeniz won't disappoint. There's something magical about dancing with the sand between your toes as the sea breeze keeps you cool.

Sugar Beach Club (Ölüdeniz): This popular venue regularly hosts beach parties with live DJs and a lively crowd. The combination of great music, delicious drinks, and a stunning beach setting makes it a night to remember.

Help Beach & Yacht Club (Fethiye): Known for its exclusive beach events, Help Beach & Yacht Club pulls out all the stops with top-notch DJs and an upscale party atmosphere. Don't miss their full-moon beach parties — they're legendary.

Çalış Beach Sunset Gatherings: While not as rowdy as some other spots, Çalış Beach offers a more laid-back beach party vibe. It's common to see people gathering with drinks, music, and good company as they watch the sun set and the stars take over the sky.

Insider Tips for Nightlife in Fethiye and Ölüdeniz

Dress Code: Most places are casual, but some upscale venues like the Yacht Club may appreciate a smarter dress code.

Happy Hours: Many bars, especially along the beach, offer happy hour deals. It's a great way to enjoy cocktails at a lower price.

Safety First: The nightlife scene here is friendly and welcoming, but it's always wise to keep an eye on your belongings and stay aware of your surroundings.

Transportation: Taxis are readily available, but if you're staying nearby, walking along the moonlit paths can be a charming way to end the night.

Local Drinks: Don't miss out on trying rakı, Turkey's beloved anise-flavored spirit. Pair it with a meze platter for a true Turkish experience.

The nightlife in Fethiye and Ölüdeniz offers something for everyone — from intimate lounges and live music venues to energetic beach parties. Whether you're looking to dance the night away or simply sip a cocktail by the sea, the energy and charm of these coastal towns will leave you with unforgettable memories. Trust me, the nights here are as magical as the days.

Shopping and Souvenirs

Shopping in Fethiye and Ölüdeniz is a delightful adventure filled with vibrant colors, exotic aromas, and intricate crafts. From bustling bazaars brimming with treasures to artisan shops offering handmade masterpieces, the shopping scene here promises a rewarding experience. Let me take you on a journey through the best places to find unique souvenirs and gifts, including those famed Turkish carpets and aromatic spices.

Traditional Turkish Bazaars: A Feast for the Senses

There's nothing quite like the lively atmosphere of a traditional Turkish bazaar. The vibrant stalls, friendly banter of shopkeepers, and endless array of goods create a sensory experience that's both fun and immersive.

Fethiye Market (Tuesday Market): The Fethiye Tuesday Market is a must-visit for anyone who loves browsing through local produce, spices, textiles, and household goods. I remember being captivated by the vibrant displays of fresh fruits and vegetables, but it was the fragrant spice stalls that truly stole the show. The market is also a great place to pick up traditional Turkish delight and dried fruits. Don't forget to haggle — it's all part of the fun!

- **Insider Tip:** Arrive early to beat the crowds and score the freshest produce and best deals.

Ölüdeniz Market (Mondays): Smaller than the Fethiye Market but equally charming, the Monday market in Ölüdeniz offers a relaxed shopping experience. You'll find a mix of local crafts, clothing, and delicious snacks. I loved sampling the freshly made gözleme (Turkish flatbread) while browsing for souvenirs.

Local Crafts and Artisan Shops: Handmade Treasures

Fethiye and Ölüdeniz are home to talented artisans who create beautiful handicrafts that reflect the region's rich cultural heritage.

Paspatur Old Town (Fethiye): Paspatur, Fethiye's charming old town, is a treasure trove of artisan shops and boutiques. As I wandered through its narrow, cobblestone streets, I discovered shops selling hand-painted ceramics, leather goods, and intricate jewelry. One shop owner even demonstrated how they crafted their silver pieces — a fascinating glimpse into traditional craftsmanship.

Nazar Boncuk Shops: You'll find plenty of shops selling *nazar boncuk* (evil eye amulets) throughout Fethiye and Ölüdeniz. These beautiful blue glass charms are said to protect against negative energy and make for meaningful souvenirs. I couldn't resist picking up a few as gifts for friends and family.

Handwoven Textiles and Scarves: Look out for shops selling handwoven textiles, including colorful scarves and table runners. The intricate patterns and high-quality craftsmanship make them perfect keepsakes.

Best Places to Buy Turkish Carpets and Spices

No trip to Turkey is complete without exploring its iconic carpets and aromatic spices.

Turkish Carpets: Works of Art Underfoot: If you're in the market for a Turkish carpet, Fethiye offers several reputable shops where you can find authentic, hand-knotted masterpieces.

- **Carpet & Kilim House (Fethiye):** This family-run store offers a stunning collection of carpets and kilims. The owner was incredibly knowledgeable, taking the time to explain the history and significance of each piece.

- **Orient Handmade Carpets (Paspatur)** Another fantastic option, this shop specializes in traditional patterns and high-quality craftsmanship. Don't be shy about negotiating the price — it's expected!

Insider Tip: Authentic Turkish carpets come with a certificate of authenticity. Always ask for one before making a purchase.

Spice Shops: Aromatic Delights: The spice stalls in Fethiye's markets are a feast for the senses.

- **Tuesday Market Spice Stalls:** Here, you'll find an impressive variety of spices, from vibrant saffron and earthy sumac to aromatic Turkish tea blends. I couldn't resist buying a bag of freshly ground Turkish coffee — the rich aroma was simply irresistible.
- **Paspatur Spice Shops:** The spice shops in Paspatur Old Town are well-stocked with beautifully packaged spices and herbal teas. They make for fantastic gifts or a way to bring the flavors of Turkey back home.

Insider Tip: Look for high-quality saffron with a deep red color. If it looks too orange or brown, it may not be authentic.

Shopping Tips for a Rewarding Experience

Haggling: Don't be afraid to negotiate, especially in markets and independent shops. Start by offering about 70% of the asking price and go from there.

Cash is King: While many places accept credit cards, having cash on hand can make transactions smoother.

Packing Souvenirs: Turkish ceramics and spices are delicate. Ask the shopkeeper to wrap them securely for travel.

Supporting Local Artisans: Seek out shops that directly support local craftspeople. It's a great way to contribute to the community while finding unique souvenirs.

Authenticity Matters: For carpets and other high-value items, always ask for a certificate of authenticity and shop from reputable sellers.

Shopping in Fethiye and Ölüdeniz is more than just a transactional experience — it's a journey through the region's vibrant culture and craftsmanship. From the bustling bazaars filled with tantalizing aromas to the artisan shops brimming with handmade treasures, there's something for everyone to discover. Trust me, whether you're hunting for a one-of-a-kind carpet or simply savoring the joy of browsing, you'll leave with more than just souvenirs — you'll take home unforgettable memories.

Sustainable Travel Tips

Traveling sustainably doesn't mean giving up comfort or excitement; it simply means being mindful of the choices we make along the way. In Fethiye and Ölüdeniz, nature's beauty takes center stage with stunning coastlines, verdant forests, and crystal-clear waters. By adopting eco-friendly practices, we can help preserve this paradise for future generations. Let me guide you through ways to make your trip as green as possible while still enjoying an unforgettable vacation.

Eco-Friendly Accommodation

One of the easiest ways to travel sustainably is by choosing accommodations that prioritize eco-conscious practices. Fortunately, Fethiye and Ölüdeniz have several fantastic options.

Green-Certified Hotels: Look for hotels with certifications such as the Green Key or other environmental accolades. These properties often use renewable energy, reduce water consumption, and implement waste management systems.

- **Yacht Boheme Hotel (Fethiye):** This chic, eco-aware hotel incorporates energy-efficient technologies and sources local, seasonal ingredients for its restaurant.

- **Perdue Hotel (Faralya)**: Nestled along the coast near Kabak Bay, Perdue Hotel focuses on minimal environmental impact while offering a serene escape surrounded by nature.

Sustainable Boutique Lodges and Eco-Resorts: Staying at smaller, locally owned accommodations often means supporting eco-friendly practices and the local economy.

- **Olive Garden Kabak**: Known for its rustic charm and eco-conscious design, this lodge uses solar power and promotes organic farming.

Tips for Eco-Friendly Stays:

- Opt for accommodations that use solar energy and water-saving techniques.
- Bring your own reusable toiletries to cut down on single-use plastics.
- Reuse towels and linens to reduce laundry water usage.

Responsible Travel Practices

Being a responsible traveler goes beyond just choosing the right hotel. It's about making thoughtful decisions every step of the way.

Mindful Waste Management: Turkey has made strides in recycling, but it's still essential to manage your waste responsibly.

- Carry a reusable water bottle; many cafes and hotels will refill it for you.
- Avoid single-use plastics by bringing a reusable shopping bag and cutlery set.
- Properly dispose of your trash, particularly in natural areas like beaches and hiking trails.

Protecting Nature and Wildlife: The stunning landscapes of Fethiye and Ölüdeniz are fragile ecosystems.

- Stick to marked trails when hiking to avoid damaging native plants.
- Don't pick wildflowers or disturb wildlife, including marine creatures.
- Never leave litter behind — if you packed it in, pack it out.

Energy and Water Conservation

- Turn off lights, air conditioning, and electronics when leaving your room.
- Limit water usage by taking shorter showers and turning off taps while brushing your teeth.

Ethical Tours and Activities: Choose tour operators that prioritize environmental conservation and ethical practices.

- Look for wildlife tours that follow ethical guidelines and don't disturb natural habitats.
- Avoid activities that exploit animals, such as dolphin shows or captive wildlife attractions.

Supporting Local Communities

Engaging with and supporting local communities is a fantastic way to make your travel experience more meaningful while contributing positively to the destination.

Shop Local: Fethiye's markets and artisan shops are filled with unique, handcrafted goods.

- Visit the Tuesday Market in Fethiye to buy fresh produce and locally made products.

- Purchase souvenirs directly from artisans, such as hand-painted ceramics, textiles, and jewelry.

Eat at Locally Owned Restaurants: Instead of dining at international chains, choose family-run eateries that serve authentic Turkish cuisine.

- Enjoy a hearty Turkish breakfast at a local café in Paspatur Old Town.
- Savor freshly caught seafood at beachfront restaurants in Ölüdeniz.

Participate in Cultural Experiences

- Take part in traditional craft workshops to learn skills like pottery or Turkish carpet weaving.
- Attend local festivals and events to immerse yourself in the region's vibrant culture.

Volunteer Opportunities: Consider giving back to the community by volunteering with local environmental or social initiatives.

Additional Sustainable Travel Tips

Offset Your Carbon Footprint: If you're flying, consider using a carbon offset program to balance out your emissions.

Public Transportation: Use mini buses (dolmuş) or rent a bike instead of relying solely on private vehicles.

Travel Light: The lighter your luggage, the lower the carbon emissions required for transport.

Eco-Friendly Souvenirs: Choose items that are sustainably made, biodegradable, or recyclable.

Traveling sustainably in Fethiye and Ölüdeniz isn't just possible — it's incredibly rewarding. By staying mindful of our impact, supporting local communities, and choosing eco-friendly options, we can ensure that this beautiful region continues to thrive for generations to come. Trust me, the memories you make will be even more meaningful knowing you've left a positive footprint behind. Let's keep this paradise pristine together!

Practical Travel Tips

Planning a smooth and stress-free trip to Fethiye and Ölüdeniz requires knowing the essentials. Let me share some practical advice to help you navigate currency matters, communicate effectively, stay safe, and enjoy peace of mind throughout your journey.

Currency and Payment Methods

Currency: The official currency in Turkey is the Turkish Lira (TRY). Banknotes come in denominations of 5, 10, 20, 50, 100, and 200 liras. Coins include kuruş (smaller units) and lira coins.

Currency Exchange:

- Currency exchange offices (döviz) are widely available in Fethiye, often offering better rates than banks.
- Avoid exchanging money at airports due to unfavorable rates.

Payment Methods:

- **Cash:** Cash is widely accepted, especially at local markets, smaller shops, and street vendors.

- **Credit and Debit Cards:** Visa and Mastercard are commonly accepted at hotels, restaurants, and larger shops. American Express is less widely used.
- **Contactless Payments:** Many places now support contactless payments via smartphones or cards.

ATMs:

- ATMs are plentiful in Fethiye and Ölüdeniz.
- Look for machines that allow withdrawals in both Turkish Lira and Euros.
- Stick to ATMs affiliated with reputable banks like Ziraat Bankası, İş Bankası, or Garanti BBVA to minimize fees.
- Notify your bank of your travel plans to avoid any card-blocking issues.

Insider Tip: Carry some small bills and coins for public transport, tips, and small purchases.

Language and Communication Tips

Official Language: The official language is Turkish, but English is widely spoken in tourist areas like Fethiye and Ölüdeniz.

Useful Phrases: Learning a few basic Turkish phrases can go a long way:

- Merhaba (Hello)
- Teşekkür ederim (Thank you)
- Lütfen (Please)
- Ne kadar? (How much?)
- Tuvalet nerede? (Where is the restroom?)

Communication Apps:

- **Google Translate:** Handy for text and voice translation.
- **Turkish Phrasebook Apps:** These can be helpful for common phrases and pronunciations.

SIM Cards and Mobile Data:: If you plan to stay connected on the go, consider purchasing a local SIM card from providers like Turkcell, Vodafone, or Türk Telekom. You'll find them at airports and in Fethiye town.

- **Insider Tip:** Look for mobile plans that offer a combination of calls, texts, and data at reasonable rates.

Health and Safety Advice

Health Precautions:

- No vaccinations are required for entry, but it's wise to stay up-to-date with routine shots.
- Drink bottled water rather than tap water.
- Pack a basic travel first-aid kit with essentials like pain relievers, antihistamines, and motion sickness tablets.

Medical Services:

- Pharmacies (eczane) are well-stocked and have knowledgeable staff.
- Fethiye has several private medical centers and public hospitals that cater to tourists.

Safety Tips:

- **Personal Safety:** Fethiye and Ölüdeniz are generally safe, but it's wise to follow standard precautions.
    - Keep an eye on your belongings in crowded areas.
    - Avoid isolated areas at night.

- **Beach and Water Safety:**
  - ○ Swim only in designated areas and heed lifeguard instructions.
  - ○ Be mindful of strong currents, especially at less sheltered beaches like Kidrak Beach.
- **Hiking Safety:**
  - ○ Wear appropriate footwear and carry enough water.
  - ○ Inform someone of your plans if hiking remote trails like those on the Lycian Way.

Insider Tip: Keep emergency numbers handy:

- Police: 155
- Ambulance: 112

Travel Insurance Recommendations

Importance of Travel Insurance:: Travel insurance is essential for covering unexpected events such as medical emergencies, trip cancellations, and lost belongings.

What to Look for in a Policy:

- Medical Coverage: Ensure it covers emergency medical treatment and evacuation.
- Trip Cancellation Protection: In case you need to cancel or shorten your trip.
- Baggage and Personal Belongings: Coverage for lost or damaged items.
- Adventure Activities: If you plan to go paragliding, hiking, or scuba diving, make sure these activities are included.

Reputable Travel Insurance Providers: Look for companies with a good reputation for comprehensive coverage and reliable customer service.

- **Insider Tip:** Double-check whether your credit card offers complimentary travel insurance when purchasing your trip.

By planning ahead and staying informed, you can navigate Fethiye and Ölüdeniz effortlessly, allowing yourself to focus on the stunning landscapes, rich culture, and unforgettable experiences that await you. Trust me — a little preparation goes a long way toward a stress-free and enjoyable adventure. Safe travels!

Where to Stay in Fethiye & Ölüdeniz

Choosing the perfect place to stay in Fethiye and Ölüdeniz is all about matching your preferences with the diverse range of accommodations available. Whether you're dreaming of luxury resorts, seeking charming boutique hotels, or looking for budget-friendly and family-oriented stays, there's something here for everyone. Let me guide you to some of the best options tailored to different travel styles.

Luxury Resorts: Indulge in Opulence

If you're after an upscale experience with all the bells and whistles, Fethiye and Ölüdeniz offer luxurious resorts that redefine comfort and elegance.

Liberty Lykia Resort:: This beachfront paradise boasts stunning views of the Aegean, multiple pools, a private beach, and a spa that will leave you utterly pampered. Dining options are plentiful, with several gourmet restaurants on-site.

Hillside Beach Club: Nestled in a secluded bay, Hillside Beach Club is perfect for couples seeking a romantic escape or families looking for refined relaxation. Think pristine beaches, water sports, and top-notch wellness services.

Yacht Classic Hotel: Set right by Fethiye Marina, this resort is a gem for those who love a blend of luxury and nautical charm. The infinity pool and sea-view suites are simply divine.

- **Insider Tip:** Book early during the high season (June to September) to secure the best rates and rooms with premium views.

Boutique Hotels: Charm and Character

Boutique hotels in the region are ideal for travelers looking for intimate stays with personalized service.

Perdue Hotel: Located near Kabak Bay, Perdue offers unique tented suites with spectacular sea views and an ambiance that screams tranquility. Perfect for honeymooners or anyone wanting a secluded retreat.

Yacht Boheme Hotel: This stylish hotel near Fethiye Marina has a bohemian-chic vibe with beautifully curated rooms. The rooftop bar is perfect for enjoying cocktails with stunning sunset views.

Casa Margot: Perched on a hill, Casa Margot boasts artistic touches and panoramic views of Fethiye Bay. It's an oasis for those who appreciate design and serenity.

- **Insider Tip:** Boutique hotels often have fewer rooms, so making reservations in advance is key.

Budget-Friendly Accommodation: Comfort on a Budget

Traveling on a budget doesn't mean compromising on comfort. There are plenty of wallet-friendly options that still offer great amenities.

Hotel Oludeniz: A simple yet comfortable hotel just a short walk from the famous Blue Lagoon. The lush garden and pool area are great for unwinding.

Fethiye Guesthouse: This cozy guesthouse offers clean rooms and a friendly atmosphere at a reasonable price. It's a great base for exploring Fethiye town.

Nevada Hotel & Spa: Located in Çalış Beach, Nevada Hotel provides great value with comfortable rooms, a pool, and spa services at affordable rates.

- **Insider Tip:** Look for accommodations slightly away from the main tourist hubs to snag better deals.

Family-Friendly Stays: Comfort and Fun for All Ages

Traveling with kids? You'll find plenty of accommodations that cater to families with spacious rooms and kid-friendly amenities.

Jiva Beach Resort: This all-inclusive resort at Çalış Beach offers a fantastic family-friendly atmosphere with multiple pools, a kids' club, and entertainment options.

Club Tuana Fethiye: Located in a lush garden setting, Club Tuana offers family rooms, a private beach, and plenty of activities for both kids and parents.

Orka Sunlife Resort Hotel: With water slides, multiple pools, and family suites, this resort is perfect for keeping the kids entertained while parents relax.

- **Insider Tip:** Look for hotels that offer complimentary kids' clubs and meal plans to make your stay stress-free.

No matter your travel style or budget, Fethiye and Ölüdeniz have accommodations that will make your stay unforgettable. From luxurious retreats to charming boutique hotels and family-friendly havens, finding your perfect base is part of the adventure. Trust me — waking up to those turquoise waters and breathtaking landscapes is worth every moment of planning. Happy booking!

Day Trips and Excursions

Fethiye and Ölüdeniz are breathtaking, but the surrounding region offers equally mesmerizing experiences. Embarking on day trips allows you to explore ancient ruins, serene beaches, and enchanting islands. Trust me, these excursions are well worth your time and will add unforgettable chapters to your travel story.

Dalyan and Kaunos Tombs: A Journey Through Time and Nature

Picture gliding along the tranquil Dalyan River, flanked by lush reeds and ancient history. The Dalyan and Kaunos region is a must-visit for nature lovers and history buffs alike.

Start your journey with a boat ride down the river, where you'll be captivated by the sight of the **Kaunos Rock Tombs** carved into the cliffs. These ancient Lycian tombs are awe-inspiring reminders of the region's storied past.

Don't miss the chance to take a dip in the therapeutic **Sultaniye Thermal Springs** or cover yourself in the famous **Dalyan mud baths** — a fun and rejuvenating experience.

- **Insider Tip:** Keep your eyes peeled for loggerhead turtles (Caretta caretta) as you approach **Iztuzu Beach**, one of their primary nesting grounds.

Patara Beach and Ancient City: Where History Meets Paradise

If you're craving a blend of culture and beach bliss, Patara delivers both in spades. The journey takes about an hour and a half from Fethiye, but it's worth every minute.

First, explore the **Ancient City of Patara**, a fascinating archaeological site that was once a major Lycian port. Wander through the well-preserved Roman theater, ancient baths, and the iconic triumphal arch.

After soaking in the history, head to **Patara Beach**, a sprawling 18-kilometer stretch of golden sand. It's one of the longest beaches in Turkey and offers a peaceful escape with crystal-clear waters.

- **Insider Tip:** Visit during sunset for a magical experience as the sky transforms into hues of orange and pink.

Tlos Ancient Ruins and Yakapark: A Scenic Escape into the Mountains

For a day trip that combines ancient history with natural beauty, head to Tlos, one of the oldest and most important Lycian cities. Perched on a hill with panoramic views of the surrounding valleys, Tlos is a photographer's dream.

Wander through the impressive ruins, including the fortress, Roman theater, and necropolis. The ancient rock-cut tombs are particularly striking, with their intricate carvings standing the test of time.

After exploring Tlos, make your way to Yakapark, a tranquil retreat known for its cascading water features and lush greenery. Enjoy a leisurely lunch in one of the shaded seating areas while listening to the soothing sound of waterfalls.

- **Insider Tip:** Try the freshly caught trout at Yakapark — it's a local specialty!

Göcek Islands: Sailing Through a Paradise of Hidden Bays

If the sea calls to you, a day exploring the Göcek Islands is an absolute must. Known for their pristine beauty and secluded bays, these islands are best explored by boat.

Set sail from Göcek Marina and hop from one idyllic bay to another. Swim in crystal-clear waters, snorkel to discover vibrant marine life, or simply relax on deck and soak in the stunning surroundings.

Popular stops include Yassica Island, Cleopatra's Bay, and Bedri Rahmi Bay, where you'll find ancient rock paintings.

- **Insider Tip:** Pack a picnic or enjoy a meal at one of the charming seaside restaurants on the islands.

Day trips from Fethiye and Ölüdeniz are more than just excursions; they're opportunities to delve deeper into the rich history, culture, and natural beauty of the region. Whether you're cruising along the Dalyan River, basking on Patara Beach, or exploring ancient ruins, these experiences will leave you with memories that last a lifetime. So, go ahead and venture beyond — I promise you won't regret it!

Staying Safe and Healthy

When traveling to a paradise like Fethiye and Ölüdeniz, it's easy to get caught up in the excitement of adventure and relaxation. However, ensuring a safe and healthy trip is just as important as making unforgettable memories. Whether you're lounging by the beach, hiking through ancient trails, or exploring the sea, a few precautionary steps can go a long way in keeping your vacation smooth and stress-free.

Beach and Water Safety

The turquoise waters of Ölüdeniz and Fethiye are undeniably inviting, but being mindful of water safety ensures a fun and worry-free experience.

Swimming Safely

- Always swim in designated areas with lifeguards present, especially at popular beaches like Ölüdeniz Beach and Kumburnu Beach.
- Be cautious of strong currents, particularly at the Blue Lagoon's entrance and some less sheltered coves.
- Pay attention to flag warnings:
  - Green: Safe to swim

- Yellow: Swim with caution
- Red: Dangerous conditions – avoid swimming
- If you're not a strong swimmer, consider wearing a life vest while enjoying deeper waters.
- Avoid swimming alone, especially in remote areas or after sunset.

Staying Hydrated and Sun-Protected

- The Mediterranean sun can be intense, even outside of peak summer months. Apply broad-spectrum sunscreen (SPF 30+) and reapply every two hours, especially after swimming.
- Wearing UV-protection sunglasses, a hat, and a light cover-up helps prevent heat exhaustion.
- Stay hydrated by drinking plenty of water throughout the day, particularly if you're swimming or engaging in beach activities.

Jellyfish and Marine Life

- While jellyfish sightings are rare, stings can occasionally happen. If stung, rinse the area with seawater and apply vinegar or a soothing gel. Avoid using fresh water, as it can worsen the sting.

- Be mindful of **sea urchins**, particularly in rocky swimming spots. Water shoes can help protect your feet.

Hiking and Adventure Precautions

From the breathtaking Lycian Way to the thrilling Saklıkent Gorge, Fethiye and Ölüdeniz offer some of the best outdoor adventures in Turkey. Staying safe while exploring ensures a fantastic experience without unnecessary risks.

Preparing for a Safe Hike

- Plan your route in advance and let someone know your itinerary, especially if hiking alone.
- Start early in the morning to avoid the midday heat and always bring enough water.
- Wear sturdy hiking shoes to navigate uneven trails, particularly on Kayaköy's ruins and the rugged Lycian Way.
- Carry a fully charged phone with offline maps and emergency contacts saved.

Dealing with Changing Weather Conditions

- The weather in the mountains and gorges can shift unexpectedly. Always carry a light waterproof jacket in case of sudden rain.
- Flash floods can occur in Saklıkent Gorge after heavy rainfall. If rain is forecasted, it's best to reschedule your visit.

Avoiding Wildlife Hazards

- While wildlife encounters are rare, be cautious of snakes and scorpions in dry, rocky areas. Wearing long pants and boots can help reduce risks.
- If you spot a wild animal, remain calm and give it space.

Staying Safe During Extreme Adventures

- Paragliding in Ölüdeniz is one of the most exhilarating activities in Turkey. Always book with a licensed company, check weather conditions, and follow the instructor's guidance.
- If joining a jeep safari, wear a seatbelt at all times and prepare for rough, bumpy terrain.

Emergency Contact Information

Knowing who to call in case of an emergency can provide peace of mind while traveling.

1. Important Phone Numbers in Turkey

- General Emergency: **112** (For Ambulance, Police, and Fire Services)
- Coast Guard: **158** (For water-related emergencies)
- Tourist Police (Fethiye): **+90 252 614 1067**
- Hospital (Fethiye State **Hospital**): **+90 252 614 4000**

Where to Find Medical Assistance

- **Fethiye State Hospital** and several **private clinics** cater to tourists and offer English-speaking services.
- Pharmacies (**"Eczane"** in Turkish) are widely available and can provide basic medications, first-aid supplies, and advice.
- In case of severe injury, private hospitals in Dalaman or Antalya offer specialized treatment.

Travel Insurance and Medical Coverage

- A **comprehensive travel insurance plan** that covers medical emergencies, adventure activities, and evacuation is highly recommended.
- Check whether your insurance includes paragliding, scuba diving, and hiking-related accidents, as some policies require add-ons for adventure sports.

Fethiye and Ölüdeniz are dream destinations filled with adventure, relaxation, and cultural richness. By taking simple precautions and staying informed, you can enjoy your trip without worry. Whether you're diving into crystal-clear waters, hiking ancient trails, or soaring through the skies on a paraglider, knowing how to stay safe will make your experience all the more rewarding.

Safe travels, and enjoy every moment of your Fethiye and Ölüdeniz adventure!

Sample Itineraries

Planning your trip to Fethiye and Ölüdeniz? These regions are not only renowned for their natural beauty but also for their rich cultural heritage displayed through various local events and festivals. To help you experience the best of both worlds, here are tailored itineraries for 3-day, 5-day, and 7-day stays, each highlighting opportunities to immerse yourself in the local culture and festivities.

3-Day Itinerary: A Taste of Tradition

Day 1: Arrival and Fethiye Exploration

- **Morning:** Begin your journey in Fethiye's old town, known as Paspatur. Wander through its charming streets, visit local artisan shops, and perhaps find unique souvenirs.
- **Afternoon:** Explore the Fethiye Museum to gain insights into the region's history and culture.
- **Evening:** Dine at a traditional Turkish restaurant and enjoy live folk music, immersing yourself in the local ambiance.

Day 2: Ölüdeniz and Local Festivities

- **Morning:** Head to Ölüdeniz Beach to relax and take in the stunning views.
- **Afternoon:** If your visit coincides with the **Ölüdeniz Air Games Festival** (typically held in October), witness thrilling aerial displays as paragliders and skydivers perform against the backdrop of the Blue Lagoon.
- **Evening:** Participate in festival activities, enjoy local food stalls, and mingle with both locals and visitors.

Day 3: Cultural Immersion

- **Morning:** Visit a local market to experience the hustle and bustle of daily life. Engage with vendors and sample regional delicacies.
- **Afternoon:** Explore nearby villages to observe traditional crafts and perhaps participate in a local workshop.
- **Evening:** Attend any local cultural events or performances that may be taking place.

5-Day Itinerary: Delving Deeper into Local Life

Days 1-3: Follow the 3-day itinerary above.

Day 4: Historical and Cultural Exploration

- **Morning:** Visit the ancient city of Tlos to explore its ruins and learn about Lycian history.
- **Afternoon:** Stop by Yakapark, a tranquil spot known for its natural beauty and traditional Turkish hospitality.
- **Evening:** If available, attend a local music or dance performance to further immerse yourself in the culture.

Day 5: Festival Fun

- **All Day:** Depending on the time of year, participate in local festivals such as the Fethiye Culture and Arts Festival, which showcases a variety of cultural events, including art exhibitions, music performances, and traditional dances.

7-Day Itinerary: A Comprehensive Cultural Journey

Days 1-5: Follow the 5-day itinerary above.

Day 6: Coastal and Cultural Excursion

- **Morning:** Take a boat trip to the Göcek Islands, enjoying the serene beauty and perhaps visiting local fishing villages.
- **Afternoon:** Explore the cultural aspects of the islands, such as local crafts and traditions.
- **Evening:** Return to Fethiye and relax at a local café, soaking in the evening atmosphere.

Day 7: Leisure and Reflection

- **Morning:** Visit a traditional Turkish bath (hamam) for a relaxing experience.
- **Afternoon:** Spend time at leisure, perhaps revisiting favorite spots or exploring new areas.
- **Evening:** Enjoy a farewell dinner featuring traditional Turkish cuisine and reflect on the vibrant cultural experiences of your trip.

Note: Festival dates can vary annually. It's advisable to check the local event calendars closer to your travel dates to plan accordingly.

By following these itineraries, you'll not only witness the natural beauty of Fethiye and Ölüdeniz but also immerse yourself in the rich cultural traditions that make this region truly special.

Conclusion

As I reflect on the magic of Fethiye and Ölüdeniz, I can't help but feel a sense of excitement for anyone preparing to explore this breathtaking destination. Whether you're drawn to its pristine beaches, ancient ruins, thrilling adventures, or rich culture, this region offers something truly special for every kind of traveler. From the moment you arrive, the turquoise waters, dramatic cliffs, and warm hospitality will make you feel like you've stepped into a dream.

But Fethiye and Ölüdeniz are more than just postcard-perfect landscapes—they're places of history, adventure, relaxation, and discovery. Every moment here is an opportunity to create lasting memories, whether you're paragliding over the Blue Lagoon, hiking the legendary Lycian Way, exploring the ruins of Kayaköy, or simply unwinding on a secluded beach. The charm of this region lies in its ability to captivate both thrill-seekers and those looking for tranquility.

Making the Most of Your Journey

To truly immerse yourself in all that Fethiye and Ölüdeniz have to offer, I encourage you to venture beyond the obvious. While iconic sights like the

Ölüdeniz Blue Lagoon and Saklıkent Gorge are unforgettable, don't overlook the hidden gems—the quiet coves of Kabak Bay, the ancient whispers of Afkule Monastery, or the untouched beauty of Gemile Bay. These places offer a more personal and intimate experience of the region, one that lingers in your heart long after you leave.

For those who love **cultural exploration**, the bustling markets of Fethiye, the historic Lycian Rock Tombs, and the lively local festivals provide a rich insight into Turkish heritage. And when it comes to food, every meal is a celebration—from the sizzling kebabs and fresh seafood to the sweet, flaky baklava enjoyed at a beachfront café.

A Destination for Every Traveler

One of the greatest joys of visiting Fethiye and Ölüdeniz is its **versatility**. Whether you're a solo traveler, a couple seeking romance, a family with kids, or a group of friends in search of adventure, this region has something tailor-made for you.

- **For Adventurers**: Dive into paragliding, scuba diving, jeep safaris, and boat tours.
- **For relaxation-seekers**: Lounge on Kidrak Beach, enjoy a Turkish bath, or take a sunset cruise.

- **For history lovers**: Wander through the Telmessos Ancient Theatre or explore the ruins of Tlos.
- **For families**: Spend the day at an aqua park, explore Butterfly Valley, or enjoy safe swimming at Kumburnu Beach.

Final Words: A Journey to Remember

As you pack your bags for Fethiye and Ölüdeniz, come with an open heart and a sense of adventure. This isn't just another vacation spot—it's a place where nature and history collide, where every sunrise feels like a fresh beginning, and where the kindness of locals makes you feel at home.

No matter how long you stay, Fethiye and Ölüdeniz will leave a mark on your soul. And when the time comes to say goodbye, you'll already be dreaming of your return.

So go ahead—**immerse yourself, explore fearlessly, and make every moment count**. Fethiye and Ölüdeniz are waiting for you!

Printed in Dunstable, United Kingdom

70167599R00067